The Word for Sorrow

JOSEPHINE BALMER previous works include the poetry collection *Chasing Catullus* (2004) and the translations *Sappho: Poems and Fragments* (1992), *Classical Women Poets* (1996) and *Catullus: Poems of Love and Hate* (2004). Reviews and journalism have appeared in the *Observer*, the *Independent on Sunday*, the *Times*, the *Times Literary Supplement* and the *New Statesman*, among others. She is also reviews editor of *Modern Poetry in Translation*. Awards include a Wingate Foundation Scholarship, two Society of Authors Authors Foundation Awards, a South East Arts Writers Bursary and an Arts Council Write Out Loud Award. Chair of the Translators' Association from 2002–05, she is currently a judge for the Times Stephen Spender Prize for Poetry in Translation and has a Ph.D. by Publication in Literature and Creative Writing from the University of East Anglia. She lives in Sussex and Cornwall.

Also by Josephine Balmer

POETRY
    Chasing Catullus (2004)

TRANSLATION
    Sappho: Poems and Fragments (1992)
    Classical Women Poets (1996)
    Catullus: Poems of Love and Hate (2004)

AS EDITOR
    Rearranging the World: A Contemporary Anthology of World
        Literature in Translation (2001)

The Word for Sorrow

JOSEPHINE BALMER

SALT

CAMBRIDGE

PUBLISHED BY SALT PUBLISHING
14a High Street, Fulbourn, Cambridge CB21 5DH United Kingdom

© Josephine Balmer 2009

The right of Josephine Balmer to be identified as the
author of this work has been asserted by her in accordance
with Section 77 of the Copyright, Designs and Patents Act 1988.

Salt Publishing 2009

Printed and bound in the United Kingdom by the MPG Books Group

Typeset in Swift 9.5 / 13

ISBN 978 1 84471 510 7 hardback

Dedicated to the memory of Edward Balmer
d. Pip Ridge, Salonica, 24th April, 1918
and for my father, his namesake

Contents

Acknowledgements

Many of the poems in this collection have previously been published in the following: *Modern Poetry in Translation* (3.3 & 3.9), *Horizon*, *The Wolf*, *Norwich Papers*, *Living Classics* and *The Translator as Writer*. Thanks are due to the editors of all these publications. The project was generously supported by a Wingate Foundation Scholarship and a Society of Authors Authors Foundation Grant. Personal thanks are also due to Paschalis Nikolaou, Cliff Ashcroft, Clive Scott, Catherine Fuller, Dorothy Sym, David Constantine, Chris Hamilton-Emery and, as ever, to Paul Dunn for faith, editorial expertise and support.

I drank in your faith, your praise
and now I must drink in your tears.
So live quietly, steer clear of fame;
keep them close, your good friends.
And nurture what little now remains
of this sad refugee: Naso's name . . .

from Tristia 3.4

From first to last I lived with fear all the time, twenty-four hours
a day, not just in spasms. Sometimes you couldn't sleep for days,
so you had plenty of time to think about what might happen . . .

from Voices of Gallipoli

Preface

The Word for Sorrow came about by chance. After working simultaneously on two classically-veined projects, a translation of Catullus' shorter poems and a poetry collection, *Chasing Catullus*, I found myself drawn to Ovid's much-neglected poems of exile, *Tristia* and *Epistulae ex Ponto*, the epistolary verse written after the poet's sudden and mysterious exile from Rome to the Black Sea in CE 8. Here, it seemed, was a rare moment when the mask of classical literary artifice slips away to reveal the raw pain of the man beneath. And then fate intervened.

One rainy spring day early in 2001, I was working on some initial translations from *Tristia* using Perseus, Tufts University's online digital classical library and lexica, when an electrical storm required me to log off from the internet. Turning instead to an old second-hand dictionary, brought at a village fete as a school student, I noticed by chance an inscription on its flyleaf that I must have seen many times over the years and yet had barely registered: faded initials and surname inked on the flyleaf and a date, early in 1900. Later, I ran this name through a few internet search engines, almost on a whim. I discovered that my dictionary's original owner had been posted with the 1/1 Royal Gloucester Hussars to Gallipoli in 1915, to the Dardanelles, which Ovid had described crossing in the poem I was translating. Accounts detailing the sickness, deprivations and dangers of the Gallipoli campaign in which 50,00 Allied troops and 85,000 Turkish soldiers died, seemed reminiscent of Ovid's powerful laments about his own exile. Further searches uncovered the private diaries and letters of British soldiers on the eastern front, many of which mentioned my dictionary owner, and which, alongside the personal testimony of his daughter, with whom I made contact, all provided striking material. Soon more parallels were revealed: old newspaper photos of the regiment lined up on the now demolished Malvern Road railway station in Cheltenham just before leaving for the East, suggested parallels with Ovid's famous poem describing his last night before exile (*Tristia* 1.3., here 'Naso's Last Night'). *The Word for Sorrow* took shape, a series of poems exploring the story of an old second-hand dictionary and its owner alongside versions of the texts it was helping to translate.

Of course Gallipoli is not Tomis or vice versa. But between these two poles, poetry can make its own connections. The Allied campaign at Gallipoli aimed to push across its peninsula from the west to the straits of the Dardanelles and on to Constantinople. However, the troops—and generals—were unprepared for its inhospitable terrain, a series of steep hills and deep ravines. After a disastrous landing at Anzac Cove in April 1915, where the defending Turkish soldiers picked off the Allied troops as they leapt from their ships, the British command prepared for a second push. The Royal Gloucester Hussars, a yeomanry regiment, whose previous experience of the War had been in Home Defence, landed at Suvla Bay to the north of the peninsula on 18th August 1915 as part of the 2nd Mounted Division (their horses were left behind in Alexandria). Their orders were to march across Suvla's salt plain and take two nearby hills; in a few days, more than 5,000 British soldiers were dead. The terrible attrition of trench warfare followed, accompanied by disease, dysentery and the assault of black flies, drawn by so many unburied corpses. Soon, the RGH's 433 men had been whittled down to 81. Suvla was finally evacuated in December 1915. Today, it is a forgotten campaign, its graveyards deserted, the roads leading up to its memorials falling away from disuse.

According to Ovid, the conditions of his own exile were equally rigorous to those of the Gallipoli soldiers. Born to a wealthy family in Sulmo on the 20th March 43 BCE,[1] by CE 8, his sensual love poetry such as *Amores* or *Ars amatoria*, and his epic masterpiece, the

---

1 Information about Ovid's life is taken mostly from his apparently autobiographical poem (*Tristia* 4.10. See 'Naso's Back Story'), although one should perhaps always allow for a fair dose of literary licence.

Metamorphoses, had made him a literary sensation in Rome. And then tragedy struck. As *Tristia* outlines so vividly, the feted, urbane poet was suddenly exiled to the furthest point of the Roman empire, the bleak Black Sea city of Tomis, often identified as the modern Romanian seaport of Constanta, which Ovid depicts as a savage, uncultured place, peopled by wild Scythian tribesmen and harassed by barbarian raids as well as plagued by an inhospitable climate. The cause of this fall from grace has since been a mystery; Ovid tells us that he was banished firstly because of his 'carmen' or poetry,—too erotic, perhaps, for morally austere Augustan Rome. Secondly, Ovid tells us, he committed an 'error', an indiscretion (careful to distinguish this from a 'crime'), perhaps unwittingly caught up in some political intrigue against the emperor Augustus. Whatever the reason, tradition has it that Ovid never returned to Rome, dying in Tomis at the age of 60, ten years after his banishment.

But how could these connections be achieved? What might be the relationship between Ovid's complex and often highly stylised exile poetry and the raw poems I was writing about Gallipoli? Firstly, of course, my versions of *Tristia* were planned for a poetry collection not a 'standard' translation (Peter Green's excellent 1994 Penguin edition fills that role with aplomb). There were also practical considerations; *Tristia* contains 50 poems in all, many more than a hundred lines long, in five books. Here narrative drive proved the key; the Gallipoli poems and Ovidian renditions had to spark off each other, to hold the dramatic tension between the two as each story progressed. And so Ovid's originals are often condensed in my new versions and/or some of their line order reversed (as, for example, in 'Naso All at Sea', from *Tristia* 1.2, in order to provide a natural continuation from the end of the preceding poem). Other poems represent shorter, more impressionistic visions of their source text, for example 'Knocking at the Door' (*Tristia* 3.2). In addition to tracking Ovid's journey via my versions, I also found Ovid seeping into my Gallipoli poems. For instance, passages from *Tristia* offer prologues or codas to several poems, such as 'Naso's Plight Hits Home' or 'Dictionary Definitions' (from 3.8 and 4.2 respectively).

Elsewhere Ovid's lines ghost my original poems, either as direct quotes, as in 'Dancing in the Dark', or as borrowed images, such as the charioteer-helmsman from *Tristia* 1.4 in 'The Horses' (which also quotes the last line of Ovid's poem) or the poet's greying hair from 4.8 which creeps into 'Welcome Note'. Other poems deliberately transgress Ovid's originals such as 'Naso the Barbarian' (based on 5.7) or the last lines of 'Naso off the Shelf' (3.1).

There was also a creative purpose behind such abridgements and emendations. My aim was that presence of the Ovid poems should seem like pages from a translator's notebook, detailed sketches before the finished original; to present snap-shots of a work in progress. For this reason I have referred to the Roman poet throughout by his *cognomen* or family name Naso—the name he calls himself in his poetry—rather than the traditional Ovid, his *nomen* or clan name, in order to distinguish my character from the 'Ovid' of literary tradition, my own construct from that of the western canon.

I'd come to *Tristia* anticipating—wanting—a moving, raw expression of grief and loss, an exposition of the plight of the exiled artist. But nothing in literature—particularly not in Latin poetry—is that simple. The more I translated Ovid's verse, the more I realised that I had something far more complicated, full of literary in-jokes, knowing mythological references, jokes, puns, alongside the account of Ovid's apparent misery in Tomis—a work constantly changing register, from high tragedy to high comedy in the blink of a line.

Recent scholarship proved even more disconcerting, particularly, the theory that Ovid's account of his exile amounts to little more than an elaborate literary hoax, conjured up not in Tomis but from the comfort of his Italian country estate: 'is it to be believed?', as Ovid asks in *Tristia*, 3.10 ('Naso Sees Hell Freeze Over'), 'Well, I can but ask . . .'[2] So how to square this revised impression of *Tristia* with my poems about Gallipoli? The more I persevered, the more I under-

---

2 Certainly Tomis, if indeed Constanta, would have been temperate and, as a former Greek colony, not without cultural life. Philip Hardie's *The Cambridge Companion to Ovid* (2002: 235) provides an excellent overview of the arguments on either side.

stood that Ovid's constant changes in register were exactly what was required for *The Word for Sorrow* too. The letters home from British officers in Gallipoli were full of the same sharp changes in tone, from horror one minute to jaunty, often inane, comments the next; making the best of it, not wanting to upset loved ones with too much reality, as 'Between the Lines' reveals.

Following my approach with Ovid, I also decided to give my dictionary owner a new name—'Geoffrey'—not just to preserve his anonymity but also to widen my narrative net, to include the testaments not just of one man but of many who fought in the campaign. I was also keen to use the device of the dictionary as a jumping-off point for other layers of narrative beyond a simple Gallipoli/Tomis or text/dictionary equation: for just as Ovid's often ironic poetic voice interposes itself into his narrative, so could my own, offering a third story of discovery, the detective story running like an undercurrent beneath. And added to the journeys of Ovid and the RGH soldiers there was now mine too, exploring the battlefields of Gallipoli and the war memorials of Gloucestershire, as well as my own past —for which of us has a history family untouched by the devastation of 1914–1918?

Translation is not just a means of expressing or exploring the process of narrative but an integral part of that narrative itself. And whereas, my previous collection, *Chasing Catullus*, employed this interplay between translation and original to explore personal grief, in *The Word for Sorrow* it is a means of approaching wider, universal tragedies. Most important of all, though, are the links forged between ancient and modern, past and present, the invisible lines that connect us to often surprising points in history, finding common ground in unexpected places, celebrating the common humanity that binds us, whether we live at the beginning of the first, the twentieth or the twenty-first century CE.

JOSEPHINE BALMER

Proem: Small Town Fête

Once we'd settle for games or strung comics,
next it's cheap set-texts, grey Penguin Classics;
moth-eaten plus fours, mould-splattered DJs—
fancy dress for all tomorrow's parties—
vintage crop, windfall of record weather,
the false softness of a Sussex summer:
Golf Captains, Oddfellows, the Lions Club,
some bloke at the bar who once read Sartre,
dark, muddied paths to bring them here too fast,
slippered shuffle from house to ward to box.

And that August day, nineteen seventy-five,
a Latin lexicon pulled from dust pile,
mildewed, battered, pock-marked, ingrained by luck
for I knew then: here it was, my life match.

One: *The Journey Out*

Naso's Book Back in Rome

Go on without me, book, but with my blessing,
back to our home town, the exile trespassing
(for you're not forbidden, banned where I am barred
though scuffed, as black—and white—as my bereaved heart)
but if your page is smeared, words left undefined,
those blots are from tears and now the tears are mine.
Go on, retrace my paths, tread the streets for me,
between the lines, in the cracks, set my feet free.
And if, in the crowd, there's one, just one, who asks,
tell them: 'yes, through me he still lives, still breathes, just—
but without the good health he enjoyed before.'
Then snap shut: remember, less is always more;
you see, in this no-man's land, the soul's slow death,
my books might be read but my sins stay scarlet.
But if they're quick to judge, here's your alibi:
poetry should be drawn down from clear cold skies
not scrawled under clouds in the eye of the storm;
poetry requires calm, quiet recollection,
should taste of the stars and yet smell of the lamp
not salt-soured seas, harsh winds, rust of wintry damp.
Poetry writes without fear: words can't be coaxed
when the knife is always pricking at your throat.
Show pity, then, all critics, be indulgent:
that these lines exist is worth astonishment.
And now, my book, bid farewell to Caesar's halls—
yes, we hope for pardon, pray for swift recall
but the road is long. Hurry. For our new home
is at the known world's end, a lifetime from Rome.
I know there are Gods who can be merciful,
still I dread the hand that led me to my fall.
For I've felt the crack of skies, roar of thunder,
so I fear the storm always at my shoulder.

Hail

A dismal spring, first of a new millennium
and three weeks (so far) of relentless rain;
lines are down, Perseus can't save the day,
no help now from latinvocabdotcom.
no hope but to return to the old addiction;
I slide the book down softly from the shelf,
dustier now, with that tell-tale whiff of rot.
Sudden hail taps on the window pane —
impatient late collection, rattled box,
slap of spade on long-buried inscription —

and there, as if still fresh, on the front page,
dual initials, double-barrelled surname:
G. A. Lyneham-Forsythe, 6th January 1900
scrawled in schoolboy boredom, thunder-stiff,
blood-brown ink, faint as an old man's vein:
the bruising flare of chained sheet lightning
that flashes, strikes, then moves on
                    leaving everything changed

Naso All at Sea

sparks glitter, cloud to cloud
                    thunder clatters, Jove-loud

We're lifted up, up, to touch the stars,
plunged down, down, into Hell's black jaws,
pitched into abyss as each swell sinks
(spray stops my lips as I speak, write this).
Look around: sky and sea, sea and sky,
the one flecked white, other furrowed grey;
gales rage between, god-forsaken, fierce,
uncertain which element to serve.
I don't fear death just the way it comes —
save me now and death would be welcome.
For if sea should subside, storm be lulled —
 if I live on, I live in exile.
So why — *why?* — wish for propitious winds?
In Sarmatia this trail must end.
I pray for safe landing, far from home,
sigh that this road to hell seems too slow;
strive for Tomis, last stop of the world,
that Black Sea, ice-hard, hail-stiff, snow-whirled;
plead for my safe passage — to Tomis!

in searching out light
                    I'm staring at darkness

Dancing in the Dark

For days now I've been stumbling after,
chasing down words just beyond reach,
searching for agreement, unpicking order,
trying not to tread on toes (or feet)

to keep up, as ever, with his deft repartee:
Writing poems that no one will read,
Naso sighed, *is like dancing in the dark,*
the gesture no one sees you make—

shame I can't find it in this stiff dictionary.
Light shrinks. Ashen stars graze the Ghyll.
A half-moon teeters on to dusk-scraped sky;
Orion traced, tip-toeing into place—

the hour for logging off and standing by,
last minute searches, last chance Googles,
as lines reel down to score its faint initials
but now a Proper name, new place, new date:

Geoffrey, April, Nineteen Fifteen,
Gloucester Yeomanry off to Gallipoli
(school Latin forgotten, for now, at least),
those same shadowed steps to the East.

Naso's Last Night

Let me tell you how it was, try to remember ...

So the hour had come. I could delay no further,
the stars had whirled across the skies, Bear westered.
What else could I do, held fast by love of country?
Yet here it was: the night exile had been decreed.
How often did I rebuke those scurrying past?:
'reflect where we are going, what we leave, don't rush'
How many times did I lie, mostly to myself,
pretending I'd fixed the hour that I would set out?
Three times I reached the door, three times I was called back
as sluggish feet indulged slowed, reluctant heart.
I made those 'final' farewells in my wretchedness,
ran back for one more kiss—the last, I swore, the last.
 'Why rush?' I asked again. 'We're headed for the East:
as Carthage was destroyed, Rome must be relinquished.'
But even as I talked, still the day crept nearer;
my morning star had risen, hate-bright Lucifer.
Now I felt disengaged, raw, wrenched in two,
limb hacked from limb, bone from bone, sinew from sinew.
My wife clung around my neck as I tried to leave,
our grief intermingled, tears (and hearts) on our sleeves:
'Let me share your journey, an exile's exiled wife,
ride stowaway on your departing ship, light freight.
Caesar himself has commanded you to leave here,
for me it will be love: love will be my Caesar.'
And so she pleaded, she tried, she tried to persuade
but as so many times before, she tried in vain.
I set out, a corpse too early for its own wake,
carried out for burial, unshaven, unkempt.

Malvern Road Station, Cheltenham

I. APRIL 1915

For once let's not dwell on impending death,
scan the thumbs-up rows of grinning faces
like bone-starved worms grubbing out fresh flesh
for those who got thumbs down, didn't make it—
Wilf Barton, Tom Honey, first from the ship,
returned as cap, belt, identity disc—
a merry bunch, pleased as punch to be off;
that day of fête then cheerful letters home,
spry postcards from a holiday gone wrong:
the men and I drink weak tea now, talk Gloucs,
bullets seem like shrill birds at dawn chorus . . .
But back on the platform, between the smiles,
I spy Geoffrey, hesitant, stiff, crowd-shy,
already out with the burying party.

II. FEBRUARY 2005

I'd hoped for a single snowdrop hunched by the tracks—
Catullus' flower untouched, as yet, in the grass—
a star-chipped bloom to soothe the scar of waste,
stench of rot, almost sweet, smear of industrial estate.
But there's no hope, no art that can heal the past;
walls have been levelled, diggers come and gone.

The day fails, sky drags with unfallen snow;
the hour, already, of the plough and of the crow.
All we can do here is say nothing and move on.

The Horses

It was all very secret, very hush-hush —
no one knew where they were headed;
the only one who didn't suffer sickness,
my father was in charge of the horses . . .

A tilted world, Bear tipped upside down,
spiralling clouds like splintered spines
and shimmering on the edge of sight,
forbidden cities, unknowable lands.
Packed like meat in the stifling hold,
Geoffrey slithered across their sweaty backs;
a teetering, punch-drunk charioteer,
harnessing terror and then letting go
the reins. Seas reared, distant ranges,
fell as suddenly — heart-dark, breath-still —
to pebbled, copse-fenced Cotswold pool.

In the late-summer chill of Whitehall, Belgravia,
palsied hands paused above a rash of plans:
for what use cavalry on rocky peninsula?
Maybe swords, bayonets, might be enough —
the age-old means of flesh against flesh . . .

But how can you kill the already dead?
Lined and waiting on the shore,
warrior-ghosts of three millennia.
Now the only passage through was fear.

By the Dardanelles

I. NASO JUMPS SHIP

Just before we reached the wind-blown Bosphorus
I deserted, dropped anchor, jumped ship at Mudros,
past Hector's tomb at Troy, sad heroes' graves,
and then on to the island of Samothrace,
gateway to Hell. It's but a short trip from here
to the mainland, that rock-hard peninsula,
past Dardanelles, exotic sounding places . . .
to Tomis where my angry Lord has sent us.
My ship takes the salt road through Helles' waters;
I take the dirt road towards Bithynia.
Steadfast ship, we'll meet again soon, I swear it.
I'll beg the Gemini, revered here, fêted:
to send us swift twinned winds, speed our still twinned paths—
favour one no more and the other no less.

II. SAMOTHRACE

Bleary on the sea-line, a faint bruised fist,
from this bone-road too far to get across:
corn tossed like pikes on a pitchforked plain,
poplars for sentinels, poppies ring-fenced,
roses grown barbed in rusted petrol cans;
farms half-built—or half-demolished—
footprint of a second, hour, millennium.

The surface falters. Goats graze. Carts pass
by in a flash, time shifting on its cracks,
the call of gull, course of blood and dust.
Here's what Naso found: a world suspended,
hung in the balance: past, future, present.

Naso Sees the End of the Beginning

In every tense, each letter of this first chapter,
you'll find my hand, rough passage of its begetter;
the oceans can bear witness to my scribbling
through ice-hard December, frostbitten, shivering.
For as we proceeded through sea-pinched Isthmus,
by now on the second of exile's many ships,
I was amazed that in depths of sea—and spirit—
productivity did not weaken, far from it.
Call it madness, maybe numbness, I can't explain,
except I know all pain was lightened by such pains.
Boötes gathered in lowering clouds, darkened days
of the Bear; southern squalls drained skies of late-year rains
until ocean became ship, ship became ocean,
still I trembled over verses—of a fashion.
Yet if we should reach port, port holds yet more terror,
Ship or shore, all that awaits me now is horror;
ahead stand blood-soaked bandits on a hostile shore,
cut-throats seeped in slaughter, cruelty, constant war.
So here, again, I beg indulgence, dear reader,
if these lines should prove less than hoped—as they are.
For they're no longer written in shady gardens
where my soft couch offered support, contemplation,
but were drawn from the deep at ebb of dying year
as salt-spray blotted page, dark cerulean blur.
And so the gale roars on, outraged that I presume
to write in its threat, its uncompromising gloom.
To the storms the spoils: let this be an end to it—
an end to it all: poem first and then poet.

Business

End of empire. Dominions shrunk
to a rattled bay, world cupped in a cove.
Maps redrawn with each retreating wave;
a hundred thousand breaths held as one,
nowhere left to conquer, no other way to go . . .

We woke among islands, we didn't know where,
that night we arrived at Mudros harbour,
sun setting on the sea like opened iris flower.
Oh, the quay was such a sight, full of war-ships
(we were sorry to leave the horses in Alexandria).
Men loaded rifles, buffed shoes and bayonets;
a parson preached sharp, shrapnelled sermons
but half-way through his pleas for forgiveness
the signal came. This means going on—and business.

Two : *Landed*

Landed

I never knew blood smelt so strong...

For a prize of dirt, few square yards of scrub,
they fought like gods as soil soaked red,
shallows curdled, stagnant with corpse-shoals.

Across Suvla plain, Geoffrey's men marched out,
without maps, with no idea where to attack,
a storm-spray of chalk and dust and blood—

too dense, too dark to tell if theirs or ours.
They crawled back like ghosts, skin singed,
clothes in tatters, tongues burnt black,

press-ganged workers after abattoir nightshift;
some spoke only in whimpers, others cried
for comrades mown down by unseen scythe,

smouldering khaki all that marked the spot.
Now the dried salt lake brimmed with body parts
as if netted by fishermen's bumper catch:

Englishmen. Dead Englishmen. Hundreds of them.
We'd never seen a corpse before and here they were,
stacked like logs or mackerel on moon-blanched shore,

mouths open, eyes wide, all just staring back,
our horror reflected in each gasping, glassy face.
We thought of home. It seemed a happy place.

Naso Off the Shelf

I dreamt my book went home again,
transformed, reformed, shuddering
like Proteus on the turn, changing shape;
no longer versed in youth's green passion
but old age's brown and shrivelled hate,
bound in sadness, grief's dark script.
And I walked with it through my city's
empty squares, footsteps soft as leaf-
fall on glittering autumn streets,
unfolding the faded map of my past life:
the Forum, the Sacred Way, the Palatine,
statues, temples, stacked libraries,
where all great works, ancient or modern,
can be read by any who might seek.
Now my book, too, tried to enter
as a guard blocked its dragging feet.
On tip-toe, noses pressed on misted pane,
we saw the touch of smoothing hand
but not for us—these lines are banned.
We heard the hush of unrolled volumes
but not of ours—by far the worst exile for them:
The shame is mine, of my *Ars amatoria*;
it stains each new page, sins of their father.
I talked too long of love, that was my 'crime'
yet my 'error' was to see and not speak out.
And so my book is closed, my heart has died.
Poetry must, poetry *can* only tell the truth.
In life we have to lie to stay alive.

Between the Lines

It seems so snug here in my grave—
you can't describe it any other way:
two feet deep, piled up with earth,
cracked headstone to protect us,
a few rancid scraps of wood,
sea-salvage, to line the box,
my mackintosh on sticks for lid
(last night a five-inch centipede
decided to share my valise—
I soon made short work of it!).
Shells rattle, universe shattered,
but so far not too much damage-
one chap had his trousers blown off—
after a few hours one takes no notice.
No flies yet, well, at least, we hope
maybe because rations are so tight:
lime juice daily, tot of rum at night.
We've had a lesson in bomb-throwing
and now I am dying to have a go.
But one of us has to stay behind—
I tossed with Major Gething, lost.
The night was extraordinary, flames
soaring above the horizon like lightning
leap-frogging across stormy Wolds;
the fires of a hundred Cerney carnivals
searing the landscape, whole world lit up.
All I could do was stand and watch.
Gething killed. Wilf Barton killed.
Gething! I tossed with him and lost.
My poor Sergeant Honey dead.
I must say I feel sad about that—

so many who came from home with us.
Today we had a go back at the Turks.
Good show: I hit my bag the last two shots.
I wish you were here to see the lights.
Funny, I feel I've been under fire all my life.

Knocking at the Door

I. NASO

A shrivelled, frost-scorched land—
melting snows in spring,
tears on an exile's cheek.
Now traitor thoughts of home,
those longed-for places, creep
up on me like reckoning—
the city I have lost, the city
that still holds my heart,
has left this empty shell of me.

For days I've been knocking
at the door of my own tomb.
Death won't hand back the key.

II. GEOFFREY

He was off to hell now with a handcart,
shovel. To stumble on half-seen shapes, shrink
from each stray limb, hewn torso, severed heart;
to follow the screams like unwinding thread,
down, down, into the hill's planked labyrinth,
plundering its spoils of the almost-dead.

Those of us who came back no longer walked
with the living. We had felt Hades' breath,
our hair turned grey in that sharp blast of frost.
The Turks could drop their bleak propaganda—
'today the flies, tomorrow the vultures'—
now we weren't men but novice corpses.

Naso Writes his Own Epitaph

If on this page you detect some new hand, fresh script
I have dictated, don't fret: for I am sick—
sick, here at the end of the unknown world, half-dead
(reports of recovery exaggerated).
Here there's no rest-home, rations fit for invalid,
no one with physician's skill in pain relief;
no one to comfort, wile away convalescence
with tall tales, no friend to sit in attendance.
Stranded far away, thoughts of home creep up in vain
but most of you, dear wife, so I mouth your name,
whisper at shades, sigh at shadows: they take your shape.
Night falls, day breaks, thoughts of you a deep dull ache.
But defer grief, dear wife, until my bones are home,
find them some suburban plot, out-of-town tomb.
And for the eyes of travellers hurrying past,
carve these letters on marble sarcophagus:
HERE LIES A PLAYER :IN LIFE, IN LOVE, IN TENDERNESS —
NASO, THE POET, DESTROYED BY HIS GENIUS.
LOVERS, PASS BY, PASS BY. I PRAY YOU WON'T BEGRUDGE ME
THIS LAST REQUEST : ON NASO'S BONES TREAD SOFTLY.
Such inscription will suffice. For my books will
prove a greater, a more lasting memorial.
In these I put my trust, despite their treachery—
to restore my good name for eternity.
Still we should give the dead their due, fair offerings:
wreaths moist with tears, monuments to suffering.
For if fire consumes, condemns flesh and bone to ash,
dust remembers. It hears our step, craves our touch . . .

Among the Graves: Green Hill, Gallipoli

By a broken sign down an unmarked track,
just wide enough for horse and cart to pass,
there is a hushed grove for hollow graves.
An open-air cathedral arched by pine,
four fattened cedars as sacrificial altar,
memorial slabs lined round in pews;
a stub of stones, milk teeth, broken through
for the half-formed fighting men they sowed.
Thy Glory Shall Not Be Blotted Out
claims Tom Honey's mossed inscription.
Remembered with Honour insists Gething's.
For Wilf Barton *Thy Will be Done*—
off-the-peg words from those who never came,
pattern-book blooms, chrysanthemums, aster,
perennial guardians for bone-bare tombs;
two thousand five hundred and eighty-nine
long-broken bodies that have never been found

Back by the gate, a lone stork takes flight,
marbled butterflies brush past, 'half-mourners',
insistent, impatient to shed black for white.
I wish now I'd spoken out, roll-called the names,
taken one small thing, at least, home to Gloucs:
rosemary sprig to dry, daisy or phlox to press
between **calamitas**. *hurt* and *healed*. **consanatus.**

Naso's Plight Hits Home

Think of the first frost in autumn
when winter's chill begins to bleed
light from days, life from fallen leaves;
that now is my disease-pocked skin.
My fate takes shape like a half-blurred ghost,
a figure in the balance that must be read.
I remember people, places, customs,
my own speech (just); I know what I was,
and I know, too, what I have become.
Caesars, generals, whatever name you take,
I'm begging you, please, get me home . . .

. . . Seven hundred miles to the west
and two thousand years further on,
they'd shoot off feet, fingers, thumbs,
finish the job, if need, with bayonet
like butcher cutting up Sunday meat . . .
For the lucky ones, there might be leave;
a few days back in a child's bare room—
battered teddy, patched rabbit, still on bed,
a few wooden toys slumped on shelf—
they no longer knew or inhabited.
In Elephant Lane, Thatto Heath,
opposite my great-grandfather's house,
a lightning-pale lad no one now can name,
arrived back home, face bone-poked
as if chased from some recurrent dream.
Too late for child's play, knucklebones,
that night he curled up and cradled his gun:
a sigh exhaled on a tightly-curtained street
that shuddered, shifted, then slept on.

Digging In

After the bloodshed comes the boredom,
the digging in and the weeding out,
the bodies of the dead beneath them,
springing the soil like softest mattress.

One troop reached down so low,
they found pavements, tesserae, pots,
a city in wait like a long-held breath
until, bone-brittle, briskly shattered, lost.

And now Geoffrey was out of his depth.
senior officers missing, half the men left:
wastage to dysentery: three a day—
and when they go they don't come back . . .

At night he sniped, played tit-for-tat games,
as the space between star-meshed trenches
hollowed to the span of a Cotswold lane;
every cough, each murmuring of Turkish

as clear and crisp as twilight thrushes:
early September and the nights are chilly,
there's talk of winter, blistering snows—
did you get my letter asking for clothes?

Ours is not to wonder or to reason why
but we think of home, the light, rain-scrubbed,
falling like sanction on Ampney, Barnsley, Cerney,
and we want our British warm so badly . . .

Naso Sees Hell Freeze Over

How can I describe them, these barren places?
For as our summer passes, cold advances
and then I see: this is what winter is like—
its brutal face, a marble earth, veined with ice.
Snow lies where it falls, never sun or rain-shrunk,
hardened by wind, unbreakable, permanent.
Furs keep out the bitter cold, rough-stitched britches—
a small patch of face, that's all you'll find of us.
Ice hangs from our hair; sounds, as we move, like chimes;
beards are silvered not just with age but stiff rime.
Wine, once open, can't be poured, it stands up straight;
chip away bottle, jar, still it keeps its shape.
One lump or two? We don't sip draughts but suck chunks,
dig out water, broken shards, from frozen lakes.
Where once ships sailed, our journeys are made on foot;
rock-hard waves resound to beat of shoe, horse-hoof.
Across brave new bridges, oxen drag their carts
(is it to be believed? Well, I can but ask . . .
for falseness here has no reward, lies don't count
and eye witness should have benefit of doubt).
Dolphins are stopped mid-leap, ships' prows frozen fast;
fish are trapped, mid-glide, clinging beneath the glass.
Under winter's cover, stealth of heart-hard night,
the enemy attacks, armed for coming fight;
swift horses, sharp barbs, weapons of destruction,
raiding, looting, destroying all before them.
When the fighting stops, still we fear its terror
as the land stands idle, untouched by plough-share;
soft grapes don't shelter in tendrilled shade of vine,
ferment in dark, deep vats to sweetness of wine.
No fruit, no leaves, no trees, no place for young men—
and yet, in this wide world, here is my domain.

Hell Hole

Suddenly the flies arrived to claim their territory.
Like lovers they drank the sweat on our bodies;
we drank fly-tea, ate bully-beef-and-fly stew,
spread seething fly-jam on fly-grained bread.
They walked on the clammy heat of the living
then cooled their feet on the skins of the dead,
burst like black steam from sun-swollen corpses.
In a moment you could kill a thousand, two,
in the next they'd be back tenfold to poison us.
Our only defence: cans of malted milk, Horlicks.
Our distraction: wondering how it was for the Turks . . .

A haze-raked morning, Gallipoli, early June
and today it's hard to imagine—almost:
boats bob like mines on the stilled Aegean,
above Suvla geese rise in mortar formation,
butterflies ricochet, black on marble whites,
old footage flickering on the edge of sight.
Over breakfast sneaked from 'deluxe' hotel
I ask our guide's shy and blushing wife—
or mime somehow as we share no language—
where they're staying, what her digs are like.
She screws up her face, pinches her nose,
makes the universal sign for 'hell hole'.

Last Orders

It should be our feast day at home, village fête—
the street all lit up, stalls set out, but instead
we're pulling ticks from shirts, waiting for first shot . . .

I've been walking too long in the paths of the dead
like trench fly cooling my feet in their icy tracks—
even here, in Gloucs, my car trails a slick of blood

on frost-flayed lanes, dictionary swapped for map
and faded handbill: RECRUITS WANTED AT ONCE.
(MEN TO HAVE THE OPTION OF FOREIGN SERVICE):

'*26 joined*' scored across in flowery pencil:
pulling men not pints: Kings Head, Elliott Arms, Cerney—
lads that had known each other since the cradle

too eager to share the next stage of their journey.
Today I sip coffee in those same, morning-sad bars;
heads shake, shoulders shrug, but there's no sign,

no last orders for 26 lost and home-sick ghosts.
By the Bull at Fairford old boys in buttoned coats
and checked ties debate Afters: *custard or ice cream?*—

Wilf Barton if he'd lived, Alf Honey, Hugh Gething.
Out in the sleet-blurred square, a black van slows,
flesh for freight; back doors slide open, rattle

as butcher steps out in blooded apron, slings a pig's
half carcass across his shoulder. Stops. Then gently shifts
the weight as if carrying a comrade from battle.

Naso Lost for Words

We are all targets, we are all on our guard:
sentinels on the walls, barbarians at the gate,
as I find myself groping for rank, name, place.
Sometimes I try to talk and the words are gone;
I have unlearned speech, there is a stone on my tongue.
My ears ring, my mouth quivers with barbarian;
it seems I could write Getics, verse in Thracian.
Believe me: my Latin now is Scythian-scarred:
don't judge what my lines might weigh, just where they are.

Thread

I'm wondering now if he ever came home,
even on the Net his trail has gone cold:
Geoffrey's disappeared without a trace.
As for Naso, he's too tricky, no bloody help—
besides, I'm too distracted to translate.

On the path above the cliffs at Cape
Cornish names ring out like bells:
Carrallack, Kenidjack, Botallack,
linked like dew-sagged spiders' webs:
Boswedden, Bollowal, Boscean,
the barbarian quivering in Naso's Latin.
Along the footpath to Carn Gloose,
I stumble on a rock entrenched in the mud,
step-smoothed to an outstretched palm—
a plea for help, a hand for the dead
to pull them up, return them to men—
like the lump that's lodged in my throat,
the stone Naso has dropped on my tongue:
de-disco, didici, *to unlearn, forget* . . .

Or the Suvla pebble I pocketed like lead,
two quartz veins crossed and twined around—
a lovers' keep-safe or sorcerer's effigy,
holding in a life by the slightest of threads.

Three: *The Way Home*

Dictionary Definitions

Construct the landscape of slaughter:
lakes, hills, forts, flesh-clogged river.
The Rhine, too, fractured, splintered,
dammed with bodies and running red
with its own blood . . .

My job now to distinguish **caedes** from **cruor**;
the one *carnage, slaughter, a battle massacre*
and the other simply *blood, that which flows*
from the wound. And then there's **lugubria**
—almost comic in English—but solemn here,
of or belonging to mourning, and in the plural,
substantive, *mourning clothes, weeds for widows.*

This shroud of Latin: **amissus. mortuus.**
The dragging, leaden cloak of language:
missing in action, presumed dead.

Naso Sees Action

Let me voice it: exile, soldier—said for respite not renown;
to stop the heart, free the thought by writing it down.
For my Muse travels with me, my friend, my betrayer,
and I am drawn to her like besotted lover.
I, whose name was on all lips, the toast of Rome,
must now defend my life, what must be my home.
Now I live among wild tribes: Getae, Sauromate —
no longer safe but entrenched by wall and gate.
In youth I shunned the rigours of military service
never took up arms unless in play or at the Circus.
In my old age now I must strap on sword and shield
as my trembling hands take cold comfort of steel;
as soon as the signal sounds, shout from watch-turret,
on a greying hair of head I buckle helmet.
Our fierce enemy brandish arrows dipped in venom,
encircle the walls with snorting horse, breath frozen.
Should we dare to leave our ramparts, venture out alone,
they fall on us like wolves on sheep outside the fold.
So this is now my home, a new landscape of fear;
for all time, it seems (and more), fate has shipped me here.
And if my Muse still dances to those same old tunes,
I write for myself, read to myself: what else can I do?
To whom can I recite my verse? Who knows the steps?
Who can hear the music, follow Latin syntax?
Yet my work, at least, is safe in my own judgment—
for those who cannot read can give no assessment.
Many lines are inscribed although most are condemned—
still I send them home in the hope you will read them.

Welcome Note

At last there is a link, a line, a letter:

I have to admit that I've been better;
I feel like a rag, seedy from dysentery,
prescribed soup, Bovril—and champagne,
half a bottle, which had me half-drunk, dizzy.
But bread and butter was the greatest treat—
marvellous after hard biscuits and bully beef.
Still, men go to hospital and are never seen again;
it's a poisonous place, very full, not well run . . .

On the ship we're stacked, rotten fruit in crates,
each day the dead cleared overboard for space
to swim beside us, bandages trailed like plankton.
A lad by me, head bound, lily-pale, raved for hours,
waving his tarnished trench trowel: 'Kill the bastards!'
before swivelling round to beg a pencil from us.
We thought he wanted to scribble a last note home
but he used it for lever to ease his dressing,
gore dripping down his face in baptismal blessing.

At Alexandria they gave us clean sheets, pyjamas,
the first since landing, a lifetime ago, at Suvla.
I looked in the mirror and hardly knew myself:
an old man looking back, black hair bleached
to white. I thought of the swans by the church,
wings unfolding like ancient maps or manuscripts.
Tonight the stars were half-murmured words
sliding softly into sound after far too long.

And then one of the women sang your song.

Naso Looks to the Stars

Tell me, tell me, is she thinking of me?
Shored under these northern constellations,
I trace the Great Bear, I track the Pole Star
which climbs so high it can touch the heavens
yet never dips beneath this vast ocean—
the star which, in its course, hears all, sees all,
which knows each one of our hearts' dark secrets.
Which must be looking down now on the walls
of Rome. So search out my wife there. Tell me:
does this same soft starlight shine on her face?
Is she, too, looking up at you tonight?
Tell me, tell me, is she thinking of me?
I need to have faith in my own good faith.
The stars, fixed and fiery in this cold sky,
can't tell me more than I can tell myself.
Yes, it's *you* she is thinking of, you fool,
your name that clings for ever to her lips.
Though far from you, she loves you from afar.
My love, as troubles creep up, as you reach
to touch the cold, empty space in our bed,
is it possible that you could forget?
Night falls. Heart-break comes. Both never-ending.
Your body aches from tossing and turning.
You feel sadness? I hate to be its cause.
You do not? Yet your grief should match my own,
yearning for your lost husband, our lost home . . .
I know you *are* anguished, kind, gentle wife,
but live through this mourning, all these hardships.
Somehow there is pleasure in the pain: grief
is leavened by all our tears, is lessened.
Loyalty, love, will wash away sadness.

Among the Graves: Ampney Crucis

In a mirrored garden framed by oak and yew,
today's bitter easterly starts to shed its snow;
an exile's dream of ice-bleached Cotswold stone.
One cross for the penitent and one for the fallen —
Wilfred, son of Jane and the late Edward Barton,
eighteen men from this tiny place alone
who won't give thanks for returning home:
a shroud of snowdrops instead of saxifrage,
obtuse constellations too stubborn to fade.
For dahlias, a bank of tomb-tight daffodils,
trampled crocuses still trying to get through.
And for cricket-song the unflinching melancholy
of migrant birds blown home too early.

Is It Nothing To You All Ye Who Walk By?
Back at Suvla, known now as Kemikli Burnu —
'the bone-strewn headland' — under haze of willow,
black-veiled women are resting from the fields.
Another plough stops, shudders up fresh yield:
a shard of tibia that once knelt here in the grass,
crushed primroses, diminished morning stars.
Or finger-bone that on sermoned Sunday mornings,
traced, like sleepy new lover, this Latin lettering,
detailing hour as well as day and date of death:
decessit inter horas XII et primam nocturnas
strange, unknown as yet, waiting to be learnt.

Seeking Quarter

I. NASO

Send new orders, please: if I can't go home
then a softer place of exile, a step nearer
but far enough away from these savage foes
who count our corpses as fair plunder.
As for those who revel in the killing—
fathers sending kids for slaughter,
gods thirsting for blood-drenched altars,
sons or brothers driven by their own Furies—
they don't know it yet but they are caught here
beneath these ice-veined skies, living
under the same fallen stars as me . . .

II. GEOFFREY

For the sick of heart—or stomach—
there can be no reprieve, no respite;
a few weeks, maybe months, to recuperate
and then straight back to the fight.
For nurses, sheets, Geoffrey must pay penance,
blood-price: hurt for healing, bone for bone.
On a frost-edged November night, crescent
moon blown through the sky like bullet-hole,
the Turks hurled a note into the trench:
We can't advance, you can't advance.
What can anyone achieve? Where to go?

The Fall

That winter did it still the bullets
like soft flesh?

        The worst blizzards
on Gallipoli in decades: troops snow-balled
to stay moving, slugged down rum tots,
stood greying, ice-stiff greatcoats
like abandoned armour outside dug-outs,
warmed now by the heat of their own carcass.
For the Anzacs, it was their first fall—
so beautiful, and covering all that was not . . .

And when the thaw came, the dead rolled
back down the hills: men, pack-animals
and something in-between, unrecognisable

until the order arrived at last:
                         Retreat.
We had gone through so much together
the living and the dead. We belonged
together. By now we'd rather not leave
than not leave together. We hoped
they didn't hear our footsteps as we passed . . .

5 a.m. A world pared to bone, frost-
pinched, ice-splintered: December 20th
1915, the last boots echo on impacted paths.
The future didn't exist any more, it was all
so far away. Now there was only the past . . .

Naso's Back Story

So you can know me, what I once was—
a player in love, in tenderness:
I call Sulmo home, where cool streams glide,
ninety miles east of Rome, as crow flies.
I was born here, forty-three the date,
with the title of eques, Knight.
Though not alone: I had a brother
who was exactly twelve months older;
both of us born on March twentieth,
the feast of war, of blood-stained combats.
In time he inclined to rhetoric,
to the word-sharp Forum's cut and thrust.
Sacred art was my pleasure, my path,
as my sly Muse drew me to her task.
My father would say: 'Why waste yourself?
For even Homer died penniless.'
Swayed, I surrendered my vocation,
wrote—tried—without versification.
And so the years slipped by in silence;
we wore togas, cloaks of government.
And then, at twenty, my brother died,
and my heart too, political drive.
Soon, so it seemed, the Senate beckoned.
Instead I narrowed my ambition—
a burden too great for my shoulders.
I hadn't the strength for its rigours;
a refugee from aspiration,
as my Muse urged superannuation.
I admired the poets of our times—
for we lived among gods, songs divine . . .

And as I the old, so young poets
revered me. I soon became famous
even if still green, beard just on chin
when I performed, gave my first reading.

My heart was open, sparks set aflame,
yet no scandal polluted my name.
In youth a wife was given to me
but we were unsuited, unhappy.
The next, through no blame, fault of her own,
was not fated to be mine for long.
The best, with me through the years, was last;
married to an exile, she holds fast.
On my head now, grey outnumbers fair,
already mottling my aging hair;
for we were in my tenth Olympiad —
that makes fifty long years since my birth —
when angry emperor banished me
to Tomis, to shores of this Black Sea.
If we leave something beyond a name,
if our fragile souls survive, remain,
if my dead parents hear by the Styx,
if even there this foul charge should stick,
know this: the cause — and I never lie —
of my exile was 'error' not 'crime'.
Here, where the clash of combat echoes,
I still write, find the word for sorrow.
This is how I stay alive, stay strong,
in the light of all my hardships, wrongs.
I thank my Muse who comforts me here;
she soothes my cares, she heals my fever.
She confers rare fame while I still live,
before this light has been extinguished.
So if it can, it can be believed,
I cannot die, worms never claim me.

Among the Graves: Salonica

Lives shrunk to map, War Graves certificate
and blurred snap of a summer's day in Greece.
On a slab by the planes, far out of sight,
I'd find my father's name: Edward Balmer,
April 1918, just months from home:
my grandmother never really recovered,
in her grief she gave a guinea to those
prepared to name their first-born son for hers;
shout 'Ted' in our street, a League team answered . . .
(and in time, of course, it would have been mine
—if not for this lack of Y chromosome).
Above the trees a nimbus noses east,
on the grass beneath, shadows like flayed skins
ward away ghosts: the dead locked out. And in.

Naso the Barbarian

I see a world without culture, savage, bleak,
a world weighed by sorrow. So men become beasts
with no fear of Law; Justice vanquished in war.
Learning, commerce, tainted now by Getic burr.
My own voice is spent, this poet's coinage,
my native speech bankrupted, impoverished.
So I talk to myself, deal in borrowed words
for this doomed art, the currency of my verse.

And then, watching the tribesmen in the markets,
bartering for goods in their common language,
while I communicate by mime or gesture,
a thought occurs: who is the barbarian here?

Up for Auction (1919)

Another chance search reveals one last link
even if there's little to connect us—
beyond this dead man's lexicon, dull ink,
we'd never have spoken the same language;
for their two grand houses, Cotswold estates,
we'd be footmen or under-kitchen maids,
the servants who go in the firing line.

But wars end. It was all up for auction:
unread libraries, shuttered house and contents,
priceless collections sold for a pittance,
value unseen. And thrown in for good luck,
a box of school-books, discarded, surplus,
rattling down the drive on a dealer's cart
and out of sight. The long trail to Sussex.

The Penny Pot

And still the ghosts come back to haunt us:
you know he served twice, my grandfather,
he went back again after it was all over—

well, the marriage wasn't going so good-
to dig out the dead, a rest from the pits,
and identify the corpses, where he could.

A strong man, a skater, champion runner,
his house in Thatto Heath full of memorabilia:
spurs, knives, guns, a cartridged bandolier.

And this. For as long as I can remember
it has stood on my father's study book-case,
offering spare change for flag-wavers

and poppy-sellers, rattled collection boxes;
paper-clips, pins, tiny keys for lost valises.
Three-legged, slightly tilted, tarnished,

forged, so I'd thought, at school metal class,
boys practising before coal or glass.
Today, as I take it, inhale its stale burnish,

I can see that its cup is a spent shell-head,
and for its triple legs, three bullets sharp
as memory, pennies saved for Charon's fare;

the known, our omphalos, suddenly unfamiliar—
a Sibyl's tripod suspended in miniature,
deciphering its sulphur dreams in the dark.

Naso's Last Word

The vultures can stop tearing at this exile's flesh
or plot to scatter my ashes—at least, not yet.
Everything might be lost, only so much life left
(to feel, to suffer this sense of doom is enough).
For where's the use in stabbing at a dead man's chest?
I don't have strength—or space—for one more cut and thrust . . .

Lover or soldier, war hero, disgraced poet—
against all odds, Geoffrey came home, Naso did not;
the player, the trickster, smiling behind the mask,
teasing out the threads of sadness, refugee's path,
this twisting, transforming journey from life to art.

The Word for Sorrow

On the fly leaf I've written
my new date, my own name:
Josephine Balmer, January 6th 2005
Do we find a text or does it find us?

Two brothers caged in eastern prison,
unable to stand, cramped in darkness,
passed the years by crossing Paris
in their mind's eye: arrondissement
by arrondissement. One would pick
two points, the other would trace
the way between—a city they had visited
only on crumpled map, by fingertip.
A path they had never taken.
A path they would always tread.

Does it matter if the journey exists
only in a captive's imagination
or the arch of a writer's eyebrow?
If Naso tricked us, never left Rome;
if 'Geoffrey's' story isn't all his own?
And would I like them if we'd met:
the player-poet with an ego even
greater than his sense of grievance?

Or retired Major, double-barrelled,
Master of the Hunt, local magistrate,
for whom Latin meant status, gender,
but never learning, love, literature?
And when the old order disappeared,
let it go for the rest of us to scavenge—
the mark of power for two millennia—
leaving our speech forever scarred,
like the taint of Naso's barbarian burr,
no going back, known world changed.

And how to tell if these shades I summon
thank or curse me, condone or condemn?
If this new life isn't a new death;
if they'd hate this fresh shroud of flesh,
fret, like harbour-bound trawlermen,
for the heart-stop stench of gutted bone?

Yet once in the cemetery at Marazion
as darkness fell, a priest, surgeon
to heal the fractured Bay, make it whole,
I sensed two figures, unseen ghosts
at each shoulder, as if my ancestors
had risen from the grave at which
I'd just picked out a weed like editor
adjective or politician, statistic:
the house-maid and the labourer,
guiding my path between fallen stars
before language, semantics, divide us.

I know my words are not their words,
I know my thoughts are not their thoughts
but every past must have a present.
And their cells are now my cells
and their matter is now my matter:
sometimes rain-hewn granite, the gorse
curved, carved by moorland squalls;
sometimes ore-bled river, forged course
from Kenidjack to Cape Cornwall.

And today in Sussex it's the drizzled gulls,
risen, flagged, like a sudden thought,
from Ghyll to Weald to Down,
where ancestors aren't flesh and bone
but the musty chatter and tented laughter
of a summer's day at hospital fête:

all those months waiting for life to begin,
a restless Celt in the land of Saxon, Latin,
learning these new lines of dominion.

We none of us need a dictionary
to define the word for sorrow:
Tomis, Gallipoli, Salonica, name
upon name etched on empty graves;
date upon date end-stopped in one same year.
Or a plaque in a country cemetery
that can't even reach double figures,
Catullus' flower passed by the furrow . . .

We are all translating the same story
search same words in same thesaurus.
What drives us on, keeps us to our path,
in every version is not gain but loss.

Epilogue: *The Observer Book of Wild Flowers*

Another second-hand buy
and, once again, opening the leaf,
I find another name inscribed:
Myrtle L. Hillacre, and underneath,
even paler, *Christmas, 1945.*
Another war over, new world in bud
balsam, self-heal, forget-me-not
boots stained with berries not blood,
afternoons by a smouldering fire
common comfrey, poor man's salve,
ash on the panes like brief snow shower.

A light-dazed world for refugees, survivors.
A world for *heartsease*, naming flowers.

I may be exiled, sent far from home,
where stars litter the dark horizon
yet my name echoes like proclamation,
my hardships sound through all domains.
I will be read from sunrise to sunset;
from dawn to dusk, from east to west.
On land and sea, they will hear my words,
my sorrow mightier than any sword . . .

from *Tristia* 4.9

Occasionally I still dream about it. Yes, sometimes. But
very seldom. Mostly it's gone away now. Mostly, it's gone.

from *Voices of Gallipoli*

References and Notes

Front quotes: *Tristia* 3.4. 39–46, and from the reminiscences of Russell Weir (Shadbolt, 1988: 37).

NASO'S BOOK BACK IN ROME: *Tristia* 1.1 (edited).

smell of the lamp: A.L. Wheeler notes in his introduction to the Loeb edition of *Tristia*: 'He toiled over his work, and his verse smells of the lamp.' (1996: xxxi).

HAIL: *Perseus*: the Tufts University digital classical library and resources website.

G.A. Lyneham-Forsythe: for privacy, I have changed this name (see Preface p. xvii).

NASO ALL AT SEA: *Tristia* 1.2. (edited).

DANCING IN THE DARK: *Writing poems* ...: *Epistulae ex Ponto* 4.2.32–4.

NASO'S LAST NIGHT : *Tristia* 1.3.1–2; 47–100 (edited).

as Carthage was destroyed, Rome must be relinquished: Ovid's Latin ('Roma relinquenda est') plays on the famous cry of Cato the Elder: 'Carthage must be destroyed' ('Delenda est Carthago').

MALVERN ROAD STATION, CHELTENHAM, APRIL 1915: *a merry bunch* ...: based on the caption for a photograph which appeared in *The Gloucester Journal*, April 17th 1915.

the men and I drink weak tea ... : based on letters home from E.T. (Tim) Cripps in August 1915, then a lieutenant with the Royal Gloucester Hussars at Suvla Bay.

MALVERN ROAD STATION, CHELTENHAM, FEBRUARY 2005: *Catullus' flower* ... an image from Catullus 11, where the flower is left at a meadow's edge to be 'touched and then devoured/by the passing plough'.

THE HORSES : *It was all very secret*: based on a conversation with the dictionary owner's daughter.

A tilted world . . . : some of the images in this stanza are inspired by *Tristia* 1.4.

But how can you kill the already dead? Tristia 1.4.28.

BY THE DARDANELLES I. NASO JUMPS SHIP: *Tristia* 1.10.15–50 (edited).

Samothrace/gateway to Hell: a reference to a cave on the island, which was sacred to Hecate, a goddess of the Underworld.

exotic sounding places . . . : a rather tongue-in-cheek condensing of the Latin text which contains some 20 lines of topographical references to memorable sites between Samothrace and Tomis.

Gemini: Castor and Pollux, the protectors of sailors and travellers, worshipped on Samothrace.

NASO SEES THE END OF THE BEGINNING: *Tristia* 1.11. (edited).

BUSINESS : *We woke among islands* . . . : based on a letter by E.T. Cripps.

LANDED : based on the eye-witness accounts of Bean (1940: 679) and Ashmead-Bartlett (1928: 189–90), war diaries quoted in Carlyon (2002: 556; 585) as well as Broadbent (2005: 234).

NASO OFF THE SHELF : *Tristia* 3.1 (edited).

BETWEEN THE LINES : based on a letter by E.T. Cripps.

KNOCKING AT THE DOOR I. NASO : based on *Tristia* 3.2.

KNOCKING AT THE DOOR II. GEOFFREY : *our hair turned grey* . . . *today the flies, tomorrow the vultures* based on a conversation with the dictionary owner's daughter.

NASO WRITES HIS OWN EPITAPH : *Tristia* 3.3. (edited).

AMONG THE GRAVES : GREEN HILL : the military cemetery on Gallipoli where the (mostly unidentified) dead from the Suvla battles are buried.

NASO'S PLIGHT HITS HOME : *Think of the first frost* . . . : *Tristia* 3.8.29–32 (edited).

like butcher cutting up Sunday meat: based on reminiscences of Joe Murray (1965: 91).

Thatto Heath: a district of St Helens, Merseyside.

DIGGING IN: based on accounts collected in Carlyon (2002: 372; 360; 356).

and when they go they don't come back: from a letter home by E.T. Cripps.

NASO SEES HELL FREEZE OVER: *Tristia* 3.10. (edited).

HELL HOLE: *Suddenly the flies* . . . : based on reminiscences of Joe Gasparich (Shadbolt, 1988: 85) and Joe Murray (1965: 76), as well as letters by E.T.Cripps.

LAST ORDERS: *It should be our feast day at home* . . . : based on a letter by E.T. Cripps.

faded handbill: a poster from October 1914, announcing the Gloucestershire pubs where recruitments would take place.

NASO LOST FOR WORDS: *Tristia* 3.14.41–52

DICTIONARY DEFINITIONS: *Construct the landscape* . . . : *Tristia* 4.2.37–43 (edited).

NASO SEES ACTION: *Tristia* 4.1 (edited).

WELCOME NOTE: based on a letter by E.T. Cripps, reminiscences of Tony Fagan (Shadbolt, 1988: 21) and photographs in Broadbent (2005: 239 & 243).

black hair bleached/to white: *Tristia* 4.8.1–2.

NASO LOOKS TO THE STARS: *Tristia* 4.3.1–38 (edited).

AMONG THE GRAVES: AMPNEY CRUCIS: *Is It Nothing To You* . . . : inscription on Cirencester World War I memorial.

'the bone-strewn headland': see Carlyon (2002: 592).

decessit inter horas . . . : inscription on the tomb of Susanna Pleydell (who died between midnight and 1 a.m., July 9th, 1642), Church of the Holy Rood, Ampney Crucis

SEEKING QUARTER I. NASO: based on *Tristia* 4.4. 49–54; 61–4.

SEEKING QUARTER II. GEOFFREY: *We can't advance* . . . : quoted by Carlyon (2002: 627).

THE FALL: *The worst blizzards* . . . : based on first-person accounts collected in Carlyon (2002: 623).

so beautiful . . . : from the diary of Anzac R.A. McInnis, quoted by Carlyon (2002: 623).

We had gone through so much together . . .: based on reminiscences of Joe Gasparich (Shadbolt, 1988: 86) and anonymous quotes in Hamilton (2003: 131).

The future didn't exist anymore: based on reminiscences of Joe Murray (1965: 191–2).

Naso's Back Story: *Tristia* 4.10 (edited)

Among the Graves: Salonica: the largely forgotten Salonica campaign was fought against the Turks in Greece, Serbia, Albania and Bulgaria from 1915–18; for every death in battle, it's said, three more men died of malaria or dysentery.

War Graves certificate: the Commonwealth War Graves Commission website offers printable commemorative 'certificates' for all the 1.7 million Commonwealth soldiers buried abroad since 1914, which includes a photograph of the cemetery.

Edward Balmer: my great-uncle, who served with The King's (Liverpool), is buried at the Sarigol Military Cemetery, Kriston, 25 miles north of Thessalonika.

Naso the Barbarian: based on *Tristia* 5.7.

The Penny Pot: *he served twice* . . . : miners, like my great-grandfather, were in great demand in the army both during and after the First World War, firstly to dig out and shore up trenches and tunnels and later to recover the dead from them.

Naso's Last Word: *The vultures can stop tearing* . . .: Ovid's last known lines, *Epistulae ex Ponto*. 4.16 47–52.

The Word for Sorrow: *Catullus' flower*: see note on 'Malvern Road Station' above.

End quotes: *Tristia* 4.9.17–24., and from the reminiscences of George Skerret (Shadbolt, 1988: 54).

Sources and Resources

C.T. LEWIS: *An Elementary Latin Dictionary* (Clarendon Press, 1897).

ELLIS ASHMEAD-BARTLETT, *The Uncensored Dardanelles* (Hutchinson, 1928).

CHARLES BEAN: 'The Story of Anzac', *Official History of Australia in the War of 1914–18, Vols I & II* (Angus & Robinson, 1938).

HARVEY BROADBENT: *Gallipoli: The Fatal Shore* (Viking, 2005).

L.A. CARLYON: *Gallipoli* (Doubleday, 2002).

ROLLO CLIFFORD: *The Royal Gloucestershire Hussars: A Photographic History of the Royal Gloucestershire Yeomanry Cavalry* (Sutton, 1991).

FRANK FOX: *The History of the Royal Gloucestershire Hussars Yeomanry, 1898–1922* (Philip Allan & Co, 1923).

PETER GREEN (TRANS.): *Ovid: The Poems of Exile* (Penguin, 1994).

JILL HAMILTON: *From Gallipoli to Gaza* (Simon & Schuster, 2003).

JOSEPH MURRAY: *Gallipoli as I Saw It* (William Kimber, 1965).

S.G. OWEN (ED.): *Tristia* (Oxford Classical Texts, 1963).

MAURICE SHADBOLT (ED.): *Voices of Gallipoli* (Hodder & Stoughton, 1988).

A.L. WHEELER (ED.): *Ovid: Tristia, Ex Ponto* (Loeb Classical Library, 1924, reprinted with revisions, 1996).

Commonwealth War Graves Commission: www.cwgc.org

Diary of Edgerton Tymewell Cripps, 1915–1918: held in the Gloucestershire Archives (D4920/2/2/3/4)

Gallipoli battlefields: www.anzacsite.gov.au

Gloucestershire archives: www.gloucestershire.gov.uk/archives

Gloucestershire newspaper collections: www.gloucestershire.gov.uk/media

Royal Gloucester Hussars: www.glosters.org.uk/hussars

Perseus digital library: www.perseus.tufts.edu

World War I ('The Long, Long Trail'): www.1914–1918.net
World War I Photographs: www.ww1photos.com